The Glowing Pink

The Glowing Pink

Selected Poems

By Standing Feather

Four Windows Press
Sturgeon Bay, Wisconsin

Copyright

Acknowledgements

This book is the culmination of my encounters with ancient Muses while living in New Mexico. Only in such a place would I have been able to hear them. I would like to acknowledge RedWulf DancingBare for affirming and expanding my inherent notion of animal medicine, as well as gently guiding me through my pain.

For the inspiration to assemble the poetry into book form, I would like to offer immense gratitude to Thomas Davis (The Weirding Storm). Thank you for continuing to suggest that the poems had a voice that needed to speak and for your endless wisdom pertaining to grammar and poetic vision.

I am grateful for the Zuni Mountain Poets, who have met every Sunday for eighteen years to allow each other to reveal the depth of our souls. A special thanks to Jack Carter North for holding space for the sacred and rowing the boat with positive Chi.

For the ability to hear the songs of the earth and make poetry from them, I would like to thank my parents - Gary, Judy and Theresa. Big thanks to Zane and Will, Stephanie, Julie, Jennifer, Ethel Davis, Zuni Mountain Sanctuary, Sharron and Melani, Maqui, Penny, and the entire El Morro Community.

"Lord Leopard" was originally published in The Zuni Mountain Poets. 2012. John Carter-North, Margaret Gross, and Thomas Davis, Ed. Bloomington, Indiana: iUniverse, Inc., pp. 80-82.

The cover painting, The Glowing Pink, is by Standing Feather.

Dedication

For Zane, Will, and Wulf

Contents

Incomprehensible

A goat does not need
a knowledge of astronomy
in order to understand
the sustainability of the rising sun
and the dangers
of a dusty moon.

Beavers cut and chew trees
to understand the anger
of the river. Blinkless trout
process calculation
under the mask
of the surface.

A man who looks away
from the people
to look into himself
wants to float in the womb of the sun
and fall asleep
in the arms of the moon.

Phragmites grow stiff
above the surface of the water
and confuse creatures
in the airless bog below.
On the eastern shore, the bulrush
lifts and bends with the wind.

Women in foxholes yell
to sooth the cries of men.
The mud hardens them
into the cold of the winter sun.
Frightened eyes blink
into the mirror of the sky.

The tyrants dance triumphant
in their messiah. The people gather
in the darkness
to understand each other
and rekindle the flames
of those who smolder.

Neptune

The full moon looks feminine
and is rubbing it in.
Even the deepest magicians
struggle to transform
a middle-aged man
into a 20's french diva,
with much different protuberances –
rounded and soft
and highlighted in glitter.

The men at Stonewall
wore masks. They were
china dolls, looking firm
while treading the edge.
They unraveled
their bound spines
to cast out diamonds. Some of us
find their diamonds
and collect them like easter eggs.

I can see my diamonds
glistening in the morning
sun. None of them
can transform my adams apple
or cleft chin or collar bones
into supple and hairless
parts of velvet beauty.
Neptune can be cruel
to the delusional.

I will launch my vessel
into the thick
of the night.

The witch of november
will join me,
and we will sing about
the rigors of moral panic
and the justice of our need
to be loved by the shoreline.

Bronze Hallelujah

A wandering man
inside the neck of the cold city –
feeding black starlings
near the secret of the water's edge,
dirty coat blowing in the wind,
blue watery eyes beaming,
and walking with
great intention –
approached me.

As a boy,
he could climb into flowers
and converse deeply
with the trees. He was
a shamanic result
of nearly dying as an infant.
Now a trickster,
he ate the corks from wine bottles
and pissed his clothes.

The inside of the flowers
had seductive openings
that pulsed
and wafted their essence
into the breeze
of the morning.
Their waxy walls
dripped sweet nectar
into the trumpet center.

The trees
talked of seed spreading
from wood ducks
and rock squirrels.
The sad ones
lamented fate,
muttering at length

about where it was
they had germinated.

The man, like me,
was lost from god
and was wondering
if I had found him
again. As two souls
in communion,
we watched
the shimmer of lights
reflecting off the dark water.

The birds on the water
looked to the sky
and back to the men
again. They clucked
and chattered
about the dangers
of hawks and owls
and the deceiving glow
of the rising sun.

Mescalito

A raven broke off
from the group
to correspond with me.
The summer sun
baked the sand at my feet,
so I jumped to fly
with the bird.

Warm breezes
from the desert
chased us around
the treetops
and gathered us together
on the flanks
of the rock wall.

The scavenger bird -
neck tilted,
head feathers ruffling,
black eyes shining,
peered deeply into me
but could not see
past my ego.

Shameful, I looked away
and down into
the valley below.
I could see myself
frozen in a circle, waiting
for the life of the sun
to thaw me.

The raven cleans death
from the nurturing earth.

The sandstone
cracks and cleaves
from the great wall
to separate me from
my decay.

Watching Hedwig

Transformation shoveled backwards.
I have owned their delusion.
Smelled like it. The odor
masked a deep cutting wound,
building a finicky pressure -
underneath, where truth whispered
and wouldn't become still.
It was adamant, like jazzy percussion -
like the angry itch.

Swordfish

The wind and the rocks
know each other
intimately enough
to dance the night away,
and they understand
each other
like rivers of molten lava
would understand
the stiffness
and serenity of the stones
they leave
behind.

I have stolen glimpses
of these kinds
of truths
while intoxicated with lunacy
and stand helpless
to the beast
that drifts in
to remove them
from me -
reshuffling my stories
into the velvety
secret.

I have seen faces
in the rocks above
the crashing sea
and formed my own
stories around them,
craving them to see me
as beautiful. I have
announced myself a woman
to the ephemeral wind.

Like swordfish,
my truths disappear
into the emptiness of the blue.

The wind and the rocks
whisper their story
into us. The trees sway
with the wind
to make a song. The
lava stones generously
hold our story.
The vultures circle
above us
when we die,
before flying to roost
under the saffron moon.

Coffee Break

It is known that rodents
burrow into buried kivas
and introduce elements
that hampers the analysis
of archaeologists seeking to
transmute their lives into
the experience of those
whose worn teeth
were never free from grinding
the dusty red earth. The
scientists gather at sunrise –
sipping their steamy coffee
and discussing whether
to go ahead with the backhoe
in section 24
or dig a hand trench.

At Chaco the people
lived and died by forty,
and round bellied women everywhere
were often awakened
early – before the sun – to sip
their last breath.
The moans rang
down the canyon
before the frozen air
could trap them in silence.
Images of medicine men
with wrinkled faces
and bent fingers lifting
to the sky
draw the scientists to talk
to the local ravens.

Brandee's Night

A puff of spiraling wind
sent from the goddess
of two-spirits
blew into my face
and hooked deep
into my root.

I wanted it to be
something to be seen,
but it wore a mask.
It wanted to reveal
new beauty
as justice.

There was a woman
inside me. The mask
I wore was behind
the sun. It smelled of
old joys and ancient
rehearsals.

3:00 a.m. at the airport
with no flight
is the right place
to introduce high heels -
after the gagging white
lines.

The terminal's bare eye
showed noble
discernment to look
away from me.
Attendants assumed I
was trouble.

Something new was ripening.

Black Rosy Finches

Black Rosy Finches
sing to remind us
of things known but not
realized. There is a woman
fearful of black rosy finches.
She works the deli case
during the summer, and
winters in the tropics. One
could order a rueben
and she would deliver
a ham on rye. Under
the dappled shade
of the street side sycamores,
she peered into me one
afternoon. Above
the top of the trees,
the bottom of the sky
was pearly blue
and lowering down
upon us.

In the middle
of the unmoved city,
she grabbed my hand
to rush me across the street
and up to a dark apartment
to wake up her son Skip,
who had fallen
into the blues.
She threw the blinds open
to let the pale sun
shine on his face. Finches
gathered at the ledge
outside the window.
The light on her round face
was revealing
her karmic wheel,

rusted and shaggy
from starved intentions
and foolish
estimates.

"Get up and stop crying!
You're from New York City!"
Skip's eyes opened a crack –
a silvery shimmer of placid
hope plunged forth
and rippled away.
He groaned a segue
and softly said "everything
feels so close to me now,
sifting gravel for gold
nuggets."
Her sharp look warned me
not to be alarmed.
The sky
had lowered
fully now,
and waves of fog
floated past the
window and past
the finches.

Shimmers of light
from the open window
and whispers of chatter
from the sycamores
snuck into the room.
The woman mumbled
an old phrase
about her tardiness.
The light revealed
that she had forgotten
to sip from her own
sacred spring. The
parched, cracked mask
of her face

had solidified from
the pain of her
old rehearsals. She
rushed out, expecting
us to make love
on the couch.

Creators

On the moon
the earth is full
more than once a month.
In the sublimation
of our thin reality,
art imagines a world
of bow-legged bears
and stout dogs
of the heart.
Our music and chants
bring integrity
to our suffering
and promise
to our children.

Crows at the Window

I.

The chilly morning and the cold sun
would slowly burn its way
into the darkened place
deep inside
the forest he longed to be now,
to say his prayer,
and he would weep and cuss and ask
anyone out there who might love him
to listen to his human pain
and help him release
the dead and dying inside him.

As a boy he could access
these dark hollows anytime,
just with his thoughts - and when
the cold autumn winds
blew his father into a rage
and would gust deep into his mother's spine
and freeze her throat,
they would all stiffen away from each other,
and he would visit the crest of the hollow
and wait for the sun rays to light up the softness
of the pine needles below.

The boy was gone now,
lost long ago inside the forest
of the ancient clay mothers
and the old trees
that protect young boys
from energies that damn them
for imagining to be little girls –
and with the ancient ones
the boys dance just as before,
when the two-spirits were loved
by their own brothers.

II.

The chilly morning rose,
and the man finished stumbling
from his dreams into the pale light
of his loveless room. The crows
at his window cawed to him
and bantered and questioned him
about his truth and order
and what might be underneath
all he was willing to see
and hear about himself -
and his own decaying laws.

This morning
he longed to find the hollows
of his youth. He would wander into
the deepest and darkest
of these places
to confirm that they contained love,
and cared for the secrets
that kept humanity from losing time
against rhythms that rise
from the deep wells
of projected fear.

III.

A Raven watched the man
rise up to crest the mesa
and move deep into the heart
of the wilderness. His grandfather
once called to him on a chilly morning
and when he arrived the old bird shared
that all the earth's creatures
are bound together, and all of it
could be ripped apart
if the people wanted to birth away
from her holy bosom.

The Raven watched the man descend
into that dark place
and remembered his own kin,
how the ones who had flown with rigidity
saw a god in themselves
and had set with yesterday's sinking sun.
They had died stiffly on the rocks below,
and the vultures would descend
from the shadowy slivers along the rimrock
to clean away possibility
from the rotting flesh.

They died bound to the rocks
and the gravity of their oldness.
The Raven croaked his croak
and lifted from the edge into the wind
and into the blue
of the boundless sky. Tonight,
when the vultures leave
the hollows,
he will ascend high into the air,
a formidable black against
the indignance of the night sky.

Fluidity

Jellyfish are creatures
dependent on movement
for the sustenance
of their life,
while having no ability
to move on their own.

The sea
inhales and exhales
in harmony with the moon.
River's tumble
from distant mountains
to hold tempo for the sway.

Lord Leopard

In the morning, before the sun,
when the earth is purple
and the stillness of the pines
prepares the mountain
for its morning song,
retreating creatures of the night
pause amongst the soft needles
to hear things. From inside
the stillness, some of them
heard the woman wake,
and begin to stoke her fires.

Birds flew down from haunted roosts
and onto her back porch to hop
and chatter and bear witness
to each other having made it
through the doubt of the night.
She opened the back door
as the retreating spiders
moved into their daytime gardens.
The sun and the spiders
were the songs
of her long dead husband.

She remembered him
as a conductor of music
and had always felt his spider webs
when the sun crested the notch
on lighting ridge. She once told
her daughter this –
and her daughter, looking troubled,
could only ask her
why she was wearing
a bone mask
with elk fur around its hollow eyes.

The morning light of september

and the hopping and scratching
of the birds
spread her memories deeper,
and she recalled the townspeople
jeering and sneering at her,
and naming her a witch.
They looked away from her.
That year, at harvest time,
the woman left her crop
to rot away on the vine.

Tonight, at sunset,
she would go outside again -
after stoking her fire
and covering herself
in her masks
to romp in the spider gardens
and to creep with the creatures
that hear so well at night.
She would slither
under the harvest moon, along
her winding paths, and maybe further.

She spent the day humming
various symphonic movements
while staring out at the blowing leaves
and changing skies. The birds flittered
in and out of the junipers,
and she recalled
watching the ants one day in august.
They scurried into their mounds
minutes before the hail had come
to damage her tomato
and datura plants.

On another summer day,
she crawled out at sunrise
and dropped to her knees,
this time wearing her leopard mask.
In the dappled light of morning

she quietly snuck the paths
between her lush gardens,
moaning and purring
until the birds left her porch sanctuary.
Above her, honeybees gathered nectar
from the sweet cleome.

When the sun was above her
she rolled around on her back
and recalled
Franz Kafka had said that
the leopards break into the temple
and drink the sacrificial chalices dry;
this occurs repeatedly,
again and again;
finally it can be reckoned upon beforehand
and becomes part of the
ceremony.

As the sun sank under windy ridge,
she placed a mask of La Luna
on top of her face.
The birds flew to the safety
of the craggy trees.
The moon had spun
a beautiful web for her,
reached down to wrap her,
whispered to her of silky nights.
Tomorrow she will awaken
to harvest her garden again.

Mouse Shaman

Elephants have come to wander about
the shrinking plain, seeking sanctuary
on shiny new paths
their ancestors would have died on.
Matriarchs guide their clans
noiselessly through the bush,
drawing maps and throwing them out
and drawing more. Their memories
of ancient paths now blocked
are swept away when they shuffle
their nervous feet.

Long ago, a mother elephant
smiled like the mona lisa
while walking through the lying lions,
never placing the second foot down
until the first was solid in its place.
Now her daughter is a thief in the night,
reluctantly poised to rob her children
of the gifts given to her
by grandmothers of the past.
Her crystal ball trunk
sways across the red road.

People gather inside the shrinking bush
to drum and pray
until thick darkness
covers the land and covers
the rows of corn. Then they turn their ears
to the dark night, and arm themselves
with firecrackers and machetes,
wide-eyed at the low rumble
of the elephants. They yell
and run and roar their power
at the beasts.

On the edge of this performance
sits a man who remembers
his grandfather had trained mice
to scamper among
the feet of elephants.
Under the purple of the african night,
the old shaman
would sneak through the bush
towards the great herds,
mice in his pockets,
softly singing his songs.
He held sacred space for the people.

The mice, the shaman, and the elephants
would have a reckoning
on the clearing's edge,
and the old bulls would charge and spit.
Long ago, the people
would drum and sing
beyond the stars,
until the moon was crimson.
Trickles of smoke from soft fires
would carry prayers into the light
of the new day.

Strata

Below the desert floor
lies a golden forest,
and the creatures there
can gaze upwards
into the light
of their headless
universe.

Beneath silken panties
and blankets of velveteen,
a young cross-dresser
has the hope yet inside
to float aloft
on fragile gossamer
wings.

Black and leafless trees
are hunched over
beneath the giants
of the golden forest. Their
trunks are trombones
for baby birds
to sing.

Behind a nervous smile,
an aging cross-dresser
plays roulette
with a mirror
and sifts through
wordless volumes of
dusty muse.

The red trumpet flowers
inside the golden forest
lean and bow
to one another
like the queens of soul.

The deepness of their glow
herald their decay.

The elder madame
of the tall girl's parade
is a flower
from the golden forest.
She has sprung forth
from the seeds of her
shame.

The Hermit

A cobalt blue tarantula
deep in the jungle
sits motionless
at the back of the burrow,
dug so rounded
to fit against her back
and constructed
with bumps of earth
that vibrate and speak
with bumps of earth
outside of her nest -
that her legs can feel
when pulled
from the deepness
of her thoughts
and into the speed
of her deadly movements.

She is a cosmic hermit -
ever aware,
spinning silk to mark time
within her lair
and within herself.
Her memories are carried
in her leg hairs
and stored in her carapace
of cloaks. She knows
of the struggles
of all those around her,
and she listens
and knows
what is trapping
and suffocating them -
and disappointing
their souls.

She hears the cries
of the world
and sits motionless for weeks
to process and weave
what the others cannot
bring themselves
to think about. They
see those around them
as strangers
and cannot feel a web
to support them.
The grandmother spider
remembers to weave
the webs of her pain
and move them
to the outside edges
of her doorway.

The morning dew
drips life into the depth
of the shadowy
burrow. The gentle
canyon wind
has blown the silk
from the doorway.
The spider has tiny lights
in her eight
black eyes,
and they illuminate
the dark spaces
of our suffering.
Her eyes are the stars
that cast light
into the blackness
of the universe.

Shapeshifter

The blues must spring
from the long space
between breaths. They
juggernaut from
holding spaces
in the throat,
only to be swallowed
back down into our pain
again.

I walked down a giant
stone tongue
in the desert southwest
and saw an old man
in a dry and dusty suit
dreaming to a place
he had never been. His
breath pushed slow
and heavy.

Birds and lizards by the water
and drums and horns
in the village below pulsed
and swayed in the sun
and the breeze
of the morning. The man
beckoned me to him,
down under the shade
in the cool sand.

I told him I knew nothing.
Unconcerned, he
licked his lips and spoke
softly of his childhood
and his mother yelling to him
about catching cold
in the frozen world

and throwing him
the patterned gray scarves.

Under the oak, his breath
was rhythmic and slow. The
sun and rocks outside
burned and shimmered
against the velvet carpet
of the dry stream. He
warned of stagnant water
and bad rum, and women
with tight pants.

His stories and breath
sunk deeper together, to the
turning of the leaves,
to the turning of the drums.
I asked again of knowing
nothing. In the glow
of the orange night,
the fire burned our loneliness
into the rocks.

He told me there always
came a time
to change the dream.
The stars and the universe
spun wildly above
the giant stones,
and the ancient mothers
called to wandering dreamers
of the dark night.

Emergers

For every idea
and every experience
there ever was,
there is a person
holding sacred space
for it.

Love and pain
emerge into us
like mayflies
from water to air.
Death molts away
from us.

On the river's edge,
songs of the drum
free our ancient memories.
Reflections on the surface
shimmer broken
in the current.

Underneath the water,
mayfly nymphs rise
to their transformation.
They climb
from their bodies
into the glistening sun.

They have let go
of their past
and cannot see their future.
Supple wings
rise from their old
bones.

The mayflies
hold space for themselves
only to breathe.
Hungry trout
sip emergers
floating near the surface.

Imbolc

A rose hip shining against the snow
must understand the mystery of the eye
and how to get its attention.
In a slipknot, the heart becomes involved,
casting its velvet wave deep into the body,
where it glows to reveal sublime pleasures
and unimaginable sorrows.

Dark eyed juncos hop on the snow
to investigate and peck the shiny aster seeds
blown purple from the winter winds.
They jump nervously from memories
inside their bodies. Coiled snakes
and hawk talons suffocating their ancestors
are locked inside their hips.

The sufferings inside our children
are eyes to look outward.
They gaze to settle memories
that are now floating in the mystery
and are outside of our attachments - away from
our persuasive touch. The purple aster seeds
wait under the dirt like bulls prodded at the gate.

Blue Train

The earth
at the bottom
of dark hollows
is perpetually wet.
It must contain
a stillness
that the trees
blowing bent
on the rimrock
cannot relate to.

The stiffness
of the grasses
and the dampness
of the dirt
in the stillness
of these bottoms
have manifested
slowly through
the chaos from
above.

My troubled
mind is full
of intellect.
Coltrane must have
lost his trouble
and listened to
the stillness,
like jagged rocks
listening to the roundness
of the river stones.

Sounds from the Mound

On the edge of the saddest city imaginable
I met an old baseball player. The creaking
wheels of his life were rusty and slowing,
and his eyes met mine at the end
of an overgrown alley. The muses can speak
without a word from the brain, and I asked
him if he was a brooklyn fan. He told me
he had stolen the jersey after his last game –
his last pitch.

He told me first that relaxation was a skill
and that he used to hear birds chirping
in the outfield and high up on the scoreboards
and that none of the other players
could remember such a thing
and called him crazy boy and spat on his shoes.
The birds would sing a melody when
they wanted him to throw a screwball
high and inside.

He told me that seduction is a subtle art
and about luring dimaggio and cobb to sleep
and waking them up with the wind tickling
their knees. One summer day in st. louis,
the boss's wife put her hand on his privates
and told him not to tell. He became frightened by her
and she had him removed from the team.
His nights since then had grown
louder.

In the back of the alley, and with the sun high above,
we smelled popcorn together
on the breezes of old pitt stadium
and joked about cleveland having no birds
and being gray over gray. We talked about the beauty
of children, the mystery of circus clowns
and the unwritten rules of baseball.

—

We parted with the afternoon shadows
creeping down the third base line.

I, too, have pitched my pains low and away,
trying to fool the batters around me, trying
to get ahead on every strike count.
I trotted towards home, imagining waking every day
just to play ball – to be with the fellas
and smell the perfume and the sweat and the beer.
I listened for the birds. They were silent
in the trees, dreaming of watching fastballs
from the tops of the scoreboards.

Masquerade

The painter realized
he had captured only
the stained and ravaged parts
of her soul.

The portrait had started
with a thought
and moved into its own
sentience.

Nectar

When the queen
leaves a hive
the worker bees
will follow her,
flying and buzzing
in a spiral.
Back inside
the empty space,
the sweet smell
of a thousand flowers
will live forever.

In the spring,
cold and stiff branches
thaw and begin
to reconcile agonies
and fears. Their
bound energies,
shackled tight
from winter's grip,
release to bloom
and feed
the bees.

A swarm of bees
buzzing low
over a silent pool
will cause
a ripple.
Early morning midges
seeking love
ride tiny waves
to the vastness
of the opposite
shore.

Scavenger

I saw a vulture sitting high up
on the cliff ledges
and hiked up to speak
to the bird. Near the top
my shoulders became heavy
and my heart
began to leak out its
sorrows. I looked up to see
the creature staring
into the valley below,
and its throat feathers danced
with the breezes
swirling up the canyon wall.
At the top I asked the bird to peck
at my heart. The blue day
began to form darkness
around the edges.

The vulture, when young,
had fallen from high perches
and was taken in by ravens.
There had been a hole
in his mother's nest.
It turned to look at me,
and could see that
I was unable to release
what had decayed.
It had spent its life eating those
who had become stuck
and could not feel
the sacredness of letting go.
The smooth-walled lips
of the mesa
glowed orange
in the southwest sunset.

The great bird hopped
from the ledge
and began a ceremonial procession
towards me. Waves
of an ancient sea
lapped to the rocks below,
and the ravens circled
high above.
Unfolding its wings,
the vulture clung to my chest
and lowered its head
to peer deeply
into the cage of my heart.
Guilt is an ambush
to consume the soul -
so I ripped myself open
to receive the medicine.

Two-Spirits

A lonely boy who wanders in the forest
talking and singing aloud to living things
that dwell beneath the light
gains a wisdom
outside of the restricted truths
that spook the people
into seeing the flowers and bees
as phantoms that dwell
underneath the hands of their god.

In a small village trees cover the sky.
A two-spirit girl that paints warrior faces
and wears a fig-wood penis
drinks ayahuasca
and calls on black panthers
and giant snakes
to heal the village with her songs.
The elder medicine men,
wrinkled and silent, had called to her.

In a small town a thin freckled boy
in a pink shirt
that rubs mud from his shoulders
and blood from his eyes
gains a freedom from those
that turn from their own grace.
Butterflies cannot inspire them
to concede to the beauty
in themselves.

In a pond a frog waits
for its visions to manifest.

The warm breezes
swirling through the bulrush
are phantoms
to the trees rooted underneath
the majesty of the purple mountain.
Down below, the river wears away the rocks
to expose a new truth for the people.

Procession

Birds sang
on that spring morning,
and children outside rejoiced
in their vitality. The doors
of the medical clinic were
stuck in perpetual motion,
opening and closing
with the pace of the children
and the birds.
Dementia. He remembered
the doctor's faint grin
and remembered thinking
go fuck yourself
and turned to his wife
in time to watch
the lust of her fear
snuff out the gleam in her eyes.
His failure to forget this
had swept him away.

Now at the head
of it all,
he opened his new eyes
to a sea of pines
and snow-topped mountain peaks
and glistening lakes
with lazy trout streams
that he could fish in
and take naps by,
just like he remembered
from his youth.
At mile six he remembered
his wallet in the car,
and he cursed at god –
and at failures and at lost
plans. Suddenly he thought
of mother, holding him

by the firelight, her black hair
like onyx in the glow.

At mile nine
it was getting dark.
He heard the rustle
down below
and listened to the soft voices
around him. They sang
like a choir
and beckoned him down
into the dark hollow.
He followed
the forest creatures
until he saw her eyes -
containers of the deepest love,
their compassion
giving the permission
to lay down beside them.
The song of the trees
sanctioned the dance of the
night.

Slick and moist,
her fawn emerged
from inside of her
and down to the grass
in a soft lump.
It lifted its head
to see her
and took its sacred breath.
The three of them
settled into the cold
of the soft grasses
for the night.
The stars and the moon
rolled over
the earth,
and the beings of the night
listened to the wheel

of the cosmic
machine.

Six days later
the two officers inspect
their precious find
and determine it to be
the missing car.
One used a radio
to call it in
and tell dispatch
that the man left his wallet
in the car.
The other officer walked to the edge
and looked up
at the vast expanse
of the looming mountain.
He figured the lost man,
in all his craziness,
had been swept away
by the rudeness
of the forest.

Supplication

A woman under the moon
can see trees holding up the sky.
She can sing to the spirits
and offer copal to the fire.
The trees can see the woman
looking to the sky.
The blackbirds acknowledge
the soft folds of the darkness
to be the dreams
of the twilight.

The absolver wakens
in the dark of the glowing spaces
around him. The people
release the imagination
of their guilt to him –
and relay the dreams
of their shame.
In the blackness he sees
his mother running to him,
daisies falling from her arms.

Under the radiance of the moon,
uninterested trout
can sense emerging caddis flies
floating foolishly
to the light of the surface,
and the blackness
of the river
can silently forsake
and carry away their hopes
of finding love.

Nine of Swords

I.

When shadows block out the light
and despair paddles the blood
that carries our holy rhythms,
the old witches knew
we were being asked to decide
to either lay down
and let a death proceed
or rise and accept the miracle
of our own divine grace.

They called these times
the nine of swords. When pulled
we are forced to lay upon them
and reconnect with the roots
of our truth.
Repeatedly, things that want to die
are begging to be released
back to the mother
where they can replenish the wells of love.

II.

The first sword pierced the man's throat,
and he thought of his song,
and its muffled cadence.
As a boy he knew the songs –
they were the doors to his joy
and his answer
to the mysteries
that baffled the people
around him.

He felt the second sword glide into his belly,
and all the irritating things
he could not stomach

poured like water through his soul.
He had overlooked
the process of others - and had turned away
from his own kindness.
The dryness of his intuition
fueled the fires of his anger.

The third stuck into the crown of his head,
and rays of universal light
could filter in -
had it not been for the cold
of his loneliness. Through the thickness
of the numb,
the sound of laughing children
brought him to weep,
and his cries drove the blade to its bottom.

Three swords cut through his heart.
He had sworn revenge, by god.
He hated the people
that couldn't see him
and wanted to hurt the ones that had hurt him.
Now he could see that their mistakes
were revealing to them
the hidden parts
of their path.

The wounds inside his heart were hurting
as the swords slowly turned
inside them.
They were kneading their way
into the deepest hiding places.
Inside the dark chambers
he saw that his own ruts
had not been dug out by them,
but by himself.

The seventh sword sunk into a tender place
between his eyes.
He saw them making fun

of who he was
and how he acted – and it hurt him.
He could see that their words
were like boomerangs,
punching back into them
to deepen their fear.

The eighth sword cut his manhood to ribbons
and left his sense
of who he was
scattered across the mountains of shame.
He wanted to run and find
the lost parts,
but could not merge himself
into what others
had wanted him to be. Letting go
would beckon a return.

The ninth sword plunged through the man
and into the bloody stump below.
Parts of him wanted to die.
In the universe,
allowing our truth to manifest is honored,
and love is vast.
He gripped the first sword to pull it out.
By choice and divine will
we scavenge ourselves alive.

Transvestite

Yesterday, as the light of the day
allowed the darkness from the other side
to conceal it,
and the beings of the golden forest
moved into their agreements
to let the mystery of the night
proceed without them,
the promise of a lover's moon
glowed seductively
behind the lurching mesa.
Basking in the shadows
of the sandstone wall,
I imagined that all leopards
appear to be female.

Capacity

A cougar on the back of a horse
will instigate a buck.
Ancestral memories
of disemboweled stallions
with hanging blue tongues
trigger their violent reactions.

Poetry has created enough beauty
to refill the splendor we leak out
when angry and fearful.
To be quenched by art
is in the memory
of our bodies.

Distant stars crumble,
and magnetic particles
float through space
to find us and make us whole.
Our memories combine with them
to birth another star.

The Glowing Pink

A frumpy man in a brown suit
beckoned me to the water's edge.
Ducks and geese floated away from him
as I approached, and he told me with his hands
to slow down. He was centered
on his stage. With a gesture, he proposed
that he could put me in a trance
with his flute, so I sat on the grass
to join him.

The afternoon sun and the cool breeze
met the surface of the pond
in shiny crystals, and the ducks and geese
paddled towards him again. He smiled
and pointed to a pink carnation
standing dignified among the summer grasses.
Then he summoned his flute
and told me with his face
to relax and close my eyes.

The herons on the opposite shore
spread their wings in homage
to the song of the flute,
and the sun rays slivered through their feathers
and onto the shimmer of the pond's façade.
The trance approached like a slow carriage,
and the golden leaves twirled down
from above. The mask of the pond
was awake.

The voices of the man's soul choired a psalm
that met the tempo of his tune, and the waves
spread up through the trees
and into the vastness of the sapphire sky.
He watched the geese as a boy
and had learned to breathe more fully
waiting for their descent. When they circled low

he could see himself
in the blackness of their eyes.

The voices of the song honored creatures
that may spend their entire lives inside a flower -
birthing and decaying away
without our ever having known of them,
and that universes are met and reconciled
inside spirals that stretch into time
we have not yet understood, and that all of this
can fit inside the carnation
glowing pink on the water's edge.

The honking of the geese had taught him
that music was the silence
between their notes. He was a magician
transmuting limitations. He could wrap himself
around a ripple and hold it still,
or let it go like angelic echoes
floating down through the rocky walls
of a lonely desert canyon.

www.ingramcontent.com/pod-product-compliance
Lightning Source LLC
LaVergne TN
LVHW021624080426
835510LV00019B/2747